To Jillian and Benjamin, on the occasion of
marriage, May 21, 2022. Wi...
Aunt Gretch and Uncle Fred

M000168090

OBSERVER'S NOTEBOOK

WEATHER

PRINCETON ARCHITECTURAL PRESS • NEW YORK

Wolkenformen.

1. Cirrus.

2. Cirrus.

3. Cirro-stratus.

4. Cirro-cumulus (Schäfchen).

5. Alto-stratus.

6. Alto-cumulus.

7. Strato-cumulus.

8. Nimbus.

9. Nimbus.

10. Cumulus.

11. Cumulus.

12. Cumulo-nimbus.

Meyers Konv.-Lexikon, 6. Aufl.   Bibliographisches Institut in Leipzig.   Zum Artikel ,Wolken'.

One of the most sublime experiences in nature, seen by ancients as messages from the gods, rainbows are caused by the refraction and internal reflection of light through water droplets suspended in the air. Although the physics of rainbows is very precise—your eye must be at an angle of forty-two degrees—each rainbow is unique because every observer occupies a different position; indeed, closing one eye reveals a different rainbow in each. Sometimes light is reflected twice inside raindrops, and a secondary ("double") rainbow is seen at an angle of fifty-one degrees, with the colors reversed (as if in a mirror) from the primary rainbow. Rainbows can also appear as complete circles, if seen from above, as in an airplane. In this case, observers on the ground see only the top half (arc) of the rainbow.

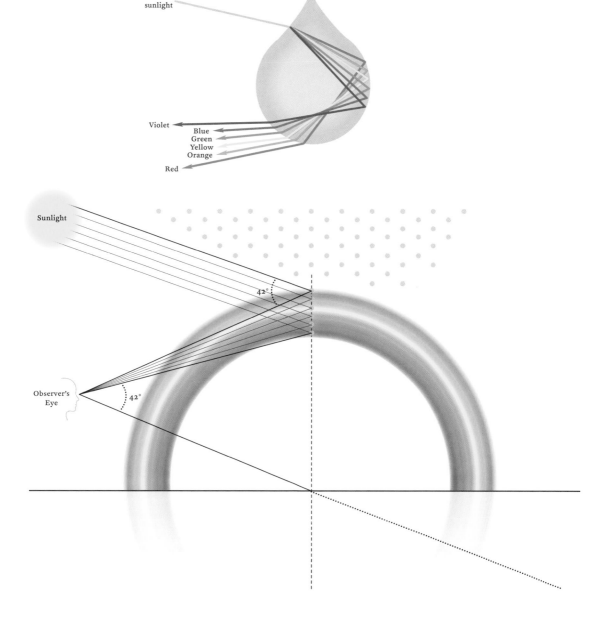

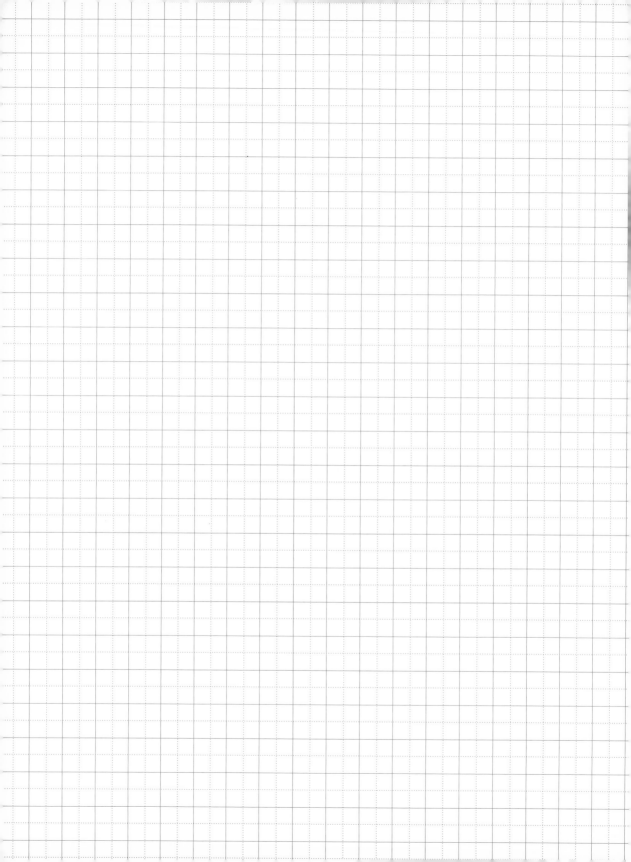

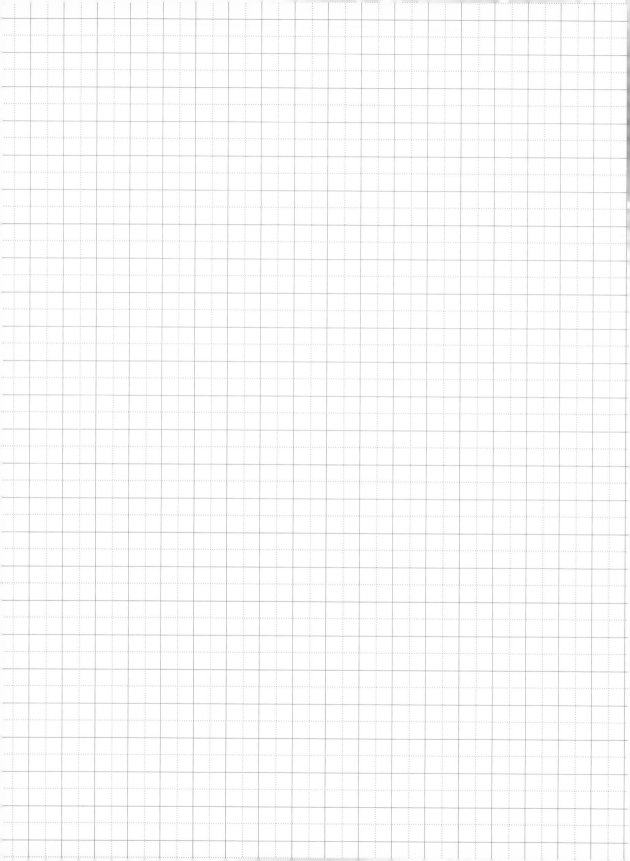

DIAGRAM OF

METEOROLOGY,

DISPLAYING THE VARIOUS PHENOMENA OF THE ATMOSPHERE.

Drawn and Engraved by John Emslie.

Published by J. Reynolds 174 Strand. Sep. 20th 1846.

REFERENCE.

1 Effects of Tempestous winds on land.
2 Effects of d.° at Sea. The Malstrom.
3 Waterspouts.
4 Fog.
5 Clouds Stratus.
6   d.° Cumulus.
7 Clouds Cirrus.
8   d.° Nimbus or rain cloud.
9   d.° Cirro Cumulus.
10 Rain.
11 Snow.
12 Perpetual Snow.
13 Glaciers.
14 Aurora Borealis.
15 Rainbow.
16 Halo.
17 Mirage.
18 Parhelia or Mock Suns.
19 Zodiacal light.
20 Ignis Fatuus or Will with a Wisp.
21 Lightning.
22 Lightning Conductor.
23 Falling Stars.
24 Aerolites.

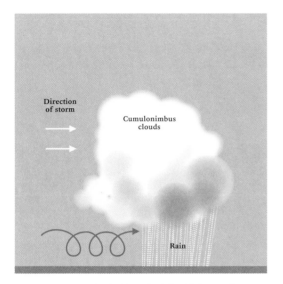

STAGE 1: Fast-moving horizontal winds roll air near the ground into a horizontal vortex.

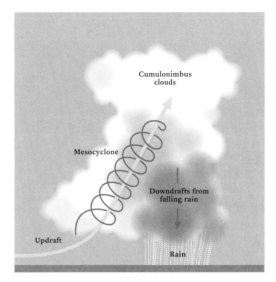

STAGE 2: Warm, moist air rises to push these spinning tubes vertically toward cool, dry air.

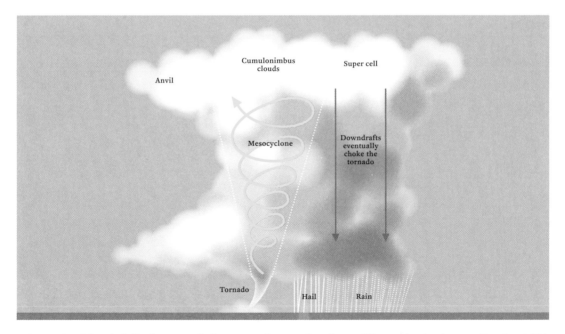

STAGE 3: A cool downdraft tilts the warm updraft, or mesocyclone, creating a "supercell," or rotating thunderstorm. Churning air high in the sky, about one-third of supercells cause rotation near the ground, forming a tornado.

GLOBAL AIR CIRCULATION

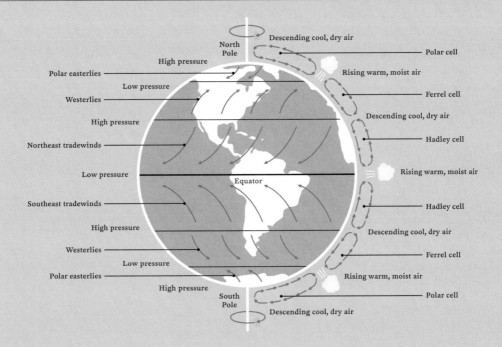

North Pole

Descending cool, dry air

Polar cell

High pressure

Polar easterlies

Rising warm, moist air

Low pressure

Westerlies

Ferrel cell

High pressure

Descending cool, dry air

Northeast tradewinds

Hadley cell

Low pressure

Equator

Rising warm, moist air

Southeast tradewinds

Hadley cell

High pressure

Descending cool, dry air

Westerlies

Ferrel cell

Low pressure

Polar easterlies

Rising warm, moist air

High pressure

Polar cell

South Pole

Descending cool, dry air

LOCAL & SEASONAL WINDS

Buran

Karaburan

Helm

Northeaster blizzards

Chinook

Mistral

Bora

Norther

Levant

Etesians

Santa Ana

Fochn

Loo

Winter monsoon

Norte

Sirocco

Amihan

Kona

Bayamo

Khamsin

Harmattan

Haboob (nondirectional)

Summer monsoon

Habagat

Berg

Brickfielder

Zonda

Sudestada

Southerly

Pampero

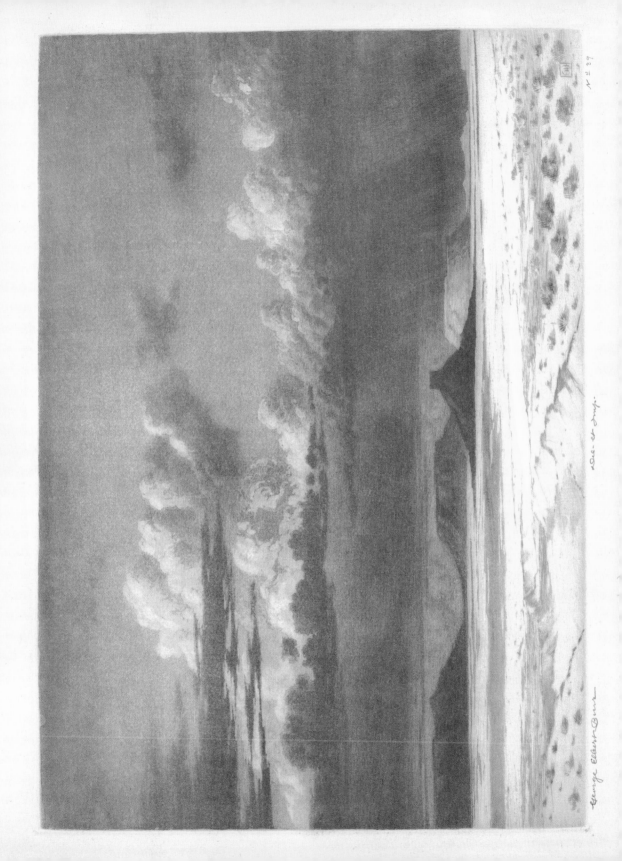

George Elliott Burr

orig. et imp.

N.° 29

George Elbert Burr, American, 1859–1939
Arizona Clouds, 20th century
Sand-paper mezzotint in color
Plate: 180 x 253 mm (7 1/16 x 9 15/16 in.)
The Fine Arts Museums of San Francisco,
California State Library long loan, A018247

WEATHER MAPPING SYMBOLS

CURRENT WEATHER

،	Intermittent drizzle
••	Continuous rain
*	Intermittent snowfall
▽	Rain shower
⁕▽	Snow shower
∿•	Freezing rain
△	Ice pellets or sleet
⌠⌠	Smoke
∞	Haze
⎰	Dust or sandstorm, no appreciable change during past hour
⫩	Funnel clouds within sight
<	Lightning visible, no thunder heard
⏉	Thunderstorm, no precipitation
•⁄⁎	Heavy thunderstorm, rain and/or snow but no hail

WEATHER FRONTS

▽▽▽▽ Cold front

●●● Warm front

●▽●▽ Stationary front

●●▽● Occluded front

WIND SPEED

◎	Calm
—	1-2 knots / 1-2 mph
—⁄	3-7 knots / 3-8 mph
—⟍	8-12 knots / 9-14 mph
—⟍⟍	13-17 knots / 15-20 mph
—⟍⟍	18-22 knots / 21-25 mph
—⟍⟍⟍	23-27 knots / 26-31 mph
—⟍⟍⟍	28-32 knots / 32-37 mph
—⟍⟍⟍⟍	33-37 knots / 38-43 mph
—⟍⟍⟍⟍	38-42 knots / 44-49 mph
—⟍⟍⟍⟍⟍	43-47 knots / 50-54 mph
—◣	48-52 knots / 55-60 mph
—◣⟍	53-57 knots / 61-66 mph
—◣⟍	58-62 knots / 67-71 mph
—◣⟍⟍	63-67 knots / 72-77 mph
—◣⟍⟍	68-72 knots / 78-83 mph
—◣⟍⟍⟍	73-77 knots / 84-89 mph
—◣◣	103-7 knots / 119-23 mph

CLOUDS

⌢	Cumulus of fair weather, little vertical development
⌂	Cumulus with vertical development
⌣	Stratocumulus
—	Stratusfractus
⏛	Cumulonimbus having a clearly fibrous (cirriform) top
⟋	Thin altostratus
⫽	Thick altostratus
⌣⌣	Thin altocumulus, mostly semitransparent
⟋⌣	Thin altocumulus, patches
⟋⌣	Altocumulus of a chaotic sky, usually at different levels
—⌐	Filaments of cirrus, or mares' tails
⌐	Dense cirrus in patches or twisted sheaves or tufts
⟋⌐	Cirrostratus not increasing and not covering entire sky
⌣⌣	Cirrocumulus

SKY COVER

○	No clouds
◑	1/10 or less
◔	2/10-3/10
◕	4/10
◐	5/10
◕	6/10
◕	7/10-8/10
◑	9/10 or overcast with openings
●	10/10 (completely overcast)
⊗	Sky obscured

Date: Location: Cloud Type(s):

Date: Location: Cloud Type(s):

Date: Location: Cloud Type(s):

Date: Location: Cloud Type(s):

Date: Location: Cloud Type(s):

Date: Location: Cloud Type(s):

Date: Location: Cloud Type(s):

Date: Location: Cloud Type(s):

Date: Location: Cloud Type(s):

Date: Location: Cloud Type(s):

Date: Location: Cloud Type(s):

Date: Location: Cloud Type(s):

Date: Location: Cloud Type(s):

Date: Location: Cloud Type(s):

Date: Location: Cloud Type(s):

Date: Location: Cloud Type(s):

Date: Location: Cloud Type(s):

Date: Location: Cloud Type(s):

WEATHER LOG

Day		Sky	Wind direction & speed	Maximum temperature	Minimum temperature	Average temperature	Humidity	
1	AM	◯						
	PM	◯						
2	AM	◯						
	PM	◯						
3	AM	◯						
	PM	◯						
4	AM	◯						
	PM	◯						
5	AM	◯						
	PM	◯						
6	AM	◯						
	PM	◯						
7	AM	◯						
	PM	◯						
8	AM	◯						
	PM	◯						
9	AM	◯						
	PM	◯						
10	AM	◯						
	PM	◯						
11	AM	◯						
	PM	◯						
12	AM	◯						
	PM	◯						
13	AM	◯						
	PM	◯						
14	AM	◯						
	PM	◯						

Dates: _____

Precipitation	Clouds	Remarks

WEATHER LOG

Day		Sky	Wind direction & speed	Maximum temperature	Minimum temperature	Average temperature	Humidity	
1	AM	◯						
	PM	◯						
2	AM	◯						
	PM	◯						
3	AM	◯						
	PM	◯						
4	AM	◯						
	PM	◯						
5	AM	◯						
	PM	◯						
6	AM	◯						
	PM	◯						
7	AM	◯						
	PM	◯						
8	AM	◯						
	PM	◯						
9	AM	◯						
	PM	◯						
10	AM	◯						
	PM	◯						
11	AM	◯						
	PM	◯						
12	AM	◯						
	PM	◯						
13	AM	◯						
	PM	◯						
14	AM	◯						
	PM	◯						

Dates: _____

	Precipitation	Clouds	Remarks

WEATHER LOG

Day		Sky	Wind direction & speed	Maximum temperature	Minimum temperature	Average temperature	Humidity	
1	AM	○						
	PM	○						
2	AM	○						
	PM	○						
3	AM	○						
	PM	○						
4	AM	○						
	PM	○						
5	AM	○						
	PM	○						
6	AM	○						
	PM	○						
7	AM	○						
	PM	○						
8	AM	○						
	PM	○						
9	AM	○						
	PM	○						
10	AM	○						
	PM	○						
11	AM	○						
	PM	○						
12	AM	○						
	PM	○						
13	AM	○						
	PM	○						
14	AM	○						
	PM	○						